Confessions
For
Living

...a handbook for a successful life

Anita Oyakhilome

LoveWorld Publications

CONFESSIONS FOR LIVING, A HANDBOOK FOR A SUCCESSFUL LIFE
ISBN - 0-9554673-0-6

Copyright © 2006 LoveWorld Publications

All Scripture quotations are taken from the King James Version of the
Bible unless otherwise indicated.

BELIEVERS' LOVEWORLD INC.
a.k.a Christ Embassy

UNITED KINGDOM
Christ Embassy Int'l Office
363 Springfield Road
Chelmsford
Essex CM2 6AW
Tel: +44 1245 490234

SOUTH AFRICA
303 Pretoria Avenue
Cnr. Harley and Hendrik Verwoerd
Randburg, Gauteng
South Africa
Tel: +27-11-326 0971, +27-11-326 0972

CANADA
101 RossDean Drive
Toronto, ON Canada M9L S6
Tel/Fax: +1-416 746 5080

GERIA
Box 13563
a, Lagos
+234-8023324188, +234-8052464131,
-1-8925724

Embassy Int'l Office
xas Dr A,
exas 75062 Tel: +1-972 255 1787

CONTENTS

HOW TO USE THIS BOOK

Establish yourself in this vital aspect of the Christian life through the following steps.

- *Read it!*

Carefully read through the chapters and spend time on enjoying the power of the scriptures.

- *Meditate it!*

As you meditate on the scriptures, see them create a change in you.

- *Confess it!*

Speak out the glorious truth of God's word and live it.

- *Announce it.* -

Light up your world with testimonies of God's goodness.

This book should inspire you make your declarations of the Word a vital aspect of your Christian lifestyle.

Chapter 1

CONFESSIONS

We having the same spirit of faith,
according as it is written, I believed,
and therefore have I spoken; we also believe,
and therefore speak; 2 Cor 4:13

Confession comes from the Greek word Homologeo. Homologeo means to declare openly by way of speaking out freely, with a deep conviction of facts. Homologeo also means being identified in thought or language with another and to confess by celebrating with praise. Confession is therefore the proclamation of that which God has said. It is speaking in unity or agreement with the Word of God. Confession also means declaring words that are consistent with God's provision, plan and purpose.

The confession referred to here should not be confused with a positive confession formula or a denial of the facts. It is not a strategy to get God to do something we desire or to get something to happen that would meet our needs. We do not chant or frame certain words in a particular order to get results. We just speak the truth of God's Word as it is. **"It is the spirit that quickeneth; the flesh profiteth nothing: the words that I speak unto you, they are spirit, and they are life"**. John 6:63

As a believer, your confession must correspond with God's Word. It must be consistent in other words; you cannot say one thing today and another thing tomorrow. Your declarations should be maintained in spite of contrary oppositions. The Bible says Abraham's faith did not weaken, even though at about one hundred years of age, the natural assumption would be that his body was as good as dead, as was Sarah's womb. He did not stagger (lose focus, entertain doubts or hesitate) at God's promise. Abraham never wavered in believing God's promise. In fact, his faith grew stronger and in this he brought glory to God. He was fully convinced that God is able to do whatever he promises.

"And being not weak in faith, he considered not his own body now dead, when he was about an hundred years old, neither yet the deadness of Sarah's womb: He staggered not at the promise of God through unbelief; but was strong in faith, giving glory to God; And being fully persuaded that, what he had promised, he was able also to perform". Romans 4: 19-21 (NIV).

This scripture gives us a clear picture of Abraham. He was a man of faith, a man of consistent faith filled declarations. He called himself the name God called him, Abraham- (the father of many). He stood on God's promise, he spoke it, he confessed it, he declared it and he lived it.

As you reflect on God's Word, there will be a transformation, a metamorphosis, a transfiguration that would produce a permanent change in your life. It will change your thinking, programme you and take you from one level of glory to another and your inner man would be strengthened by the Word.

"For this cause I bow my knees unto the Father of our Lord Jesus Christ, Of whom the whole family in heaven and earth is named, That he would grant you, according to the riches of his glory, to be strengthened with might by his Spirit in the inner man;" Ephesians 3:14-16

Sit back and let God pilot your life with His word. Be fully convinced like Abraham that God is able to do what He promised because He is faithful. God's eternal purpose for His children is for them to experience the unending flow of the supernatural everyday of their lives until they live that kind of life unconsciously.

7

YOUR TONGUE

The word is nigh thee, even in thy mouth, and in thy heart:" Romans 10:8

*Y*our tongue is a powerful weapon that can give you enormous joy and pleasure the rest of your life when used wisely; On the other hand, when used wrongly it could make your life miserable. The Bible gives a clear demonstration of the power of the tongue in James 3: 5-6. **"Even so the tongue is a little member, and boasteth great things. Behold how great a matter a little fire kindleth! And the tongue is a fire, a world of iniquity: so is the tongue among our members, that it defileth the whole body, and setteth on fire the course of nature; and it is set on fire of hell."**

Our God is confident of the words that go out of His mouth and this is clearly stated in Isaiah 55:11 "So shall my word be that goeth forth out of my mouth: it shall not return unto me void, but it shall accomplish that which I please, and it shall prosper in the thing whereto I sent it."

The centurion who came to see Jesus in Capernaum wanted help for his sick and paralyzed servant; and having a good knowledge of authority, he had just one request for Jesus. He said, "Speak the words only and my servant shall be healed." Matthew 8:8

You ought to speak boldly and with confidence and trust in the gospel of our Lord Jesus Christ. You can do this speaking to yourself in psalms and hymns and spiritual songs; making melody in your heart to the Lord. Speak to yourself and prophesy to yourself; God has given you utterance. Paul says in Ephesians 6: 19- 20 "And for me, that utterance may be given unto me, that I may open my mouth boldly, to make known the mystery of the gospel, For which I am an ambassador in bonds: that therein I may speak boldly, as I ought to speak"

The natural man is governed by his senses; the carnal man has his language; he is careless with his words. He talks like the world. He speaks the way he feels. "I have head aches, back pains, neck pains etc." The spiritual man cannot afford to speak carelessly. He is a son of the King and where the word of a king is there is power. Words are important in the spiritual arena.

A spiritual man does not speak based on his five senses, but based on the Word. He knows he cannot be sick, he cannot be discouraged and he cannot be poor. Train your mouth to speak right, speak faith not fear; speak

9

wisely not foolishly; speak pleasantly not unpleasantly and as you do so your future becomes even more beautiful.

℘ The Holy Spirit and Your Tongue ℆

The Holy Spirit is your senior partner; He is your Helper, Strengthener, Guide, Instructor and Teacher. Your life and accomplishments can be achieved with eternal values when you are totally yielded to the Holy Spirit. God has connected you to an unbeatable partnership with Himself. Being connected with Christ makes you fruitful. You are identified with Christ in your life. Jesus proudly identified with us. He is not ashamed of us. He boldly stated in John 15:5 that "I am the vine, ye are the branches: He that abideth in me, and I in him, the same bringeth forth much fruit: for without me ye can do nothing".

The Holy Spirit makes your life beautiful and exciting. One of the things the Holy Spirit does in your life as a Christian is to help you tame your tongue. You cannot make spiritual advancement irrespective of how long you have been saved if you cannot tame your tongue. You will remain a spiritual babe. Your mind must be inundated with the thoughts of the Spirit, fill your mind with God's Word continually until it becomes your way of life. Then your tongue will restore health back to you.

"There is that speaketh like the piercing of a sword: but the tongue of the wise promotes health." Proverbs 12:18 A mature Christian masters the use of his tongue.

When you are yielded to the Holy Spirit, He helps you tame your tongue. When you are completely yielded to God, you will yield your tongue to the Holy Spirit and then your prayers will be effective, because your words, prayer and praise will be consistent with God's word. And when your mind is yielded to Him by fellowship with the Spirit and submitted to the Lordship of the Word, your manner of life will reflect the character of the Spirit.

℘ Use Your Tongue ℭ

The correct use of your tongue would give you good results. Jesus came to teach us how to get results by using our tongue the right way. He said, For assuredly, I say to you, whoever says to this mountain, 'Be removed and be cast into the sea,' and does not doubt in his heart, but believes that those things he says will be done, he will have whatever he says. Mark 11:23

When the understanding of the power of the scriptures dawns on you, you will neither be sick nor yield your body to any kind of aliment again. Christ is your life as a result the life of God flows through your veins.

The Bible says in Proverbs 11:9 "... **but through knowledge shall the just be delivered**". This is not talking about science or philosophical knowledge but refers to revelation knowledge, which the Spirit of God imparts to you through the Word. Positive thinking is adopted by man's intellect because it appeals to the natural mind, but it is a flawed human copy of a divine principle of life

11

as revealed in the scriptures and is not in accordance with the bible. As much as God wants you to live in health, abundance and success, He also very much wants and expects you to live in the Word; to study His Word and live a life full of faith declarations. God's Word gives life so speak faith filled words

There is power in the words you speak and that power is released when you speak. If the Word only remains in your heart, it will not produce results; you have to speak it out. Your tongue is the key that unlocks your blessings. You put the Word of God into your spirit, believe it and let it come out of your mouth.

Consider these verses of Scripture:

"I love them that love me; and those that seek me early shall find me. Riches and honour are with me; yea, durable riches and righteousness. My fruit is better than gold, yea, than fine gold; and my revenue than choice silver." Proverbs 8: 17-19

"But his delight is in the law of the LORD; and in his law doth he meditate day and night. And he shall be like a tree planted by the rivers of water, that bringeth forth his fruit in his season; his leaf also shall not wither; and whatsoever he doeth shall prosper." Psalm 1:2, 3

"This book of the law shall not depart out of thy mouth; but thou shalt meditate therein day and night, that thou mayest observe to do according to all that is written therein: for then thou shalt make thy way prosperous, and then thou shalt have good success." Joshua 1:8

"We having the same spirit of faith, according as it is written, I believed, and therefore have I spoken; we also believe, and therefore speak;" 2 Corinthians 4:13

"But what saith it? The word is nigh thee, even in thy mouth, and in thy heart: that is, the word of faith, which we preach; That if thou shalt confess with thy mouth the Lord Jesus, and shalt believe in thine heart that God hath raised him from the dead, thou shalt be saved. For with the heart man believeth unto righteousness; and with the mouth confession is made unto salvation" Romans 10: 8 - 10

Chapter 3

THE HIGH PRIEST OF OUR CONFESSION

*Seeing then that we have
a great high priest, that is passed into
the heavens, Jesus the Son of God, let
us hold fast our profession.*

Hebrews 4:14

Jesus is the High Priest of our confession. This means Jesus is the Apostle and High Priest of our words and He is faithful to Him that appointed Him as Moses was. The name of Jesus is not ordinary. It is higher than any other name and has never lost its power. Jesus expects that we use His name with boldness and confidence, so He tells us that, **"And whatsoever ye shall ask in my name, that will I do, that the Father may be glorified in the Son. If ye shall ask any thing in my name, I will do it."** John 14: 13-14. He will fulfil His priestly responsibilities, ensuring we receive the fulfilment of God's promises as we confess and believe with our hearts, holding fast to our declarations while looking away fromsymptoms,circumstances and closed doors.

God has predestined us in Christ and has delegated His authority to us to do the same works Christ did by using His name; God sees us in Christ and has placed us in a position of authority because of the death of our Lord Jesus Christ for us. We are now seated together with Christ. The Bible say in Hebrews 8:1 *"Now of the things which we have spoken this is the sum: We have such an high priest, who is set on the right hand of the throne of the Majesty in the heavens;.."*. So our role in the kingdom is clear stand firm on our declaration of your faith irrespective of what you feel or what you see. God is faithful as promised in Hebrews 10:23 "Let us hold fast the profession of our faith without wavering; (for he is faithful that promised;)"

When you announce the works of Satan over you, you deny God's power over you, however, when you declare who you are in Christ and confess what God has done for you, you bring glory to God. Sometimes sickness, failure, frustrations and debt might try to cloud your perceptions and deny you your right as a son or daughter of God, at other times these symptoms even come with pains. It doesn't matter. Jesus is greater than them all! Stay fixed on the Word.

When you confess and maintain your confession, our High Priest Jesus Christ, acts on our behalf according to our confession of His Word and He will intercede to our Father for the benefits of the promises we confess. Maintain your confessions in Him.

15

"Surely he hath borne our griefs, and carried our sorrows: yet we did esteem him stricken, smitten of God, and afflicted. But he was wounded for our transgressions, he was bruised for our iniquities: the chastisement of our peace was upon him; and with his stripes we are healed." Isaiah 53: 4-5

"Who his own self bare our sins in his own body on the tree that we, being dead to sins, should live unto righteousness: by whose stripes ye were healed." 1 Peter 2: 24

"I am crucified with Christ: nevertheless I live; yet not I, but Christ liveth in me: and the life which I now live in the flesh I live by the faith of the Son of God, who loved me, and gave himself for me." Gal 2: 20

"Stand fast therefore in the liberty wherewith Christ hath made us free, and be not entangled again with the yoke of bondage". Gal 5: 1

"According as his divine power hath given unto us all things that pertain unto life and godliness, through the knowledge of him that hath called us to glory and virtue: Whereby are given unto us exceeding great and precious promises: that by these ye might be partakers of the divine nature, having escaped the corruption that is in the world through lust." 2 Peter 1:3-4

"But we all, with open face beholding as in a glass the glory of the Lord, are changed into the same image from glory to glory, even as by the Spirit of the Lord." 2 Corinthians 3:18

"But of him are ye in Christ Jesus, who of God is made unto us wisdom, and righteousness, and sanctification, and redemption..." 1 Corinthians 1: 30

"For we are His workmanship, created in Christ Jesus for good works, which God prepared beforehand that we should walk in them." Ephesians 2: 10

"For this cause I bow my knees unto the Father of our Lord Jesus Christ, Of whom the whole family in heaven and earth is named,". Ephesians 3:14 - 15

"Now therefore ye are no more strangers and foreigners, but fellowcitizens with the saints, and of the household of God; And are built upon the foundation of the apostles and prophets, Jesus Christ himself being the chief corner stone;" Ephesians 2:19-20 (NLT)

"Even when we were dead in sins, hath quickened us together with Christ, (by grace ye are saved;) And hath raised us up together, and made us sit together in heavenly places in Christ Jesus:." Ephesians 2: 5, 6

ॐ His Promises For You ॐ

God's promises are for your benefit. They are packed with favour and goodness for you. Every believer has an individual right to receive every blessing promised by God.

"He staggered not at the promise of God through unbelief; but was strong in faith, giving glory to God; And being fully persuaded that, what he had promised, he was able also to perform." Romans 4: 20-21

"Bless the LORD, O my soul: and all that is within me bless his holy name. Bless the LORD, O my soul, and forget not all his benefits:" Psalm 103: 1-2

"And what *is* the exceeding greatness of His power toward us who believe, according to the working of His mighty power which He worked in Christ when He raised Him from the dead and seated *Him* at His right hand in the heavenly *places*, far above all principality and power and might and dominion, and every name that is named, not only in this age but also in that which is to come. And He put all *things* under His feet, and gave Him *to be* head over all *things* to the church," Ephesians 1: 19-22

"And being made perfect, he became the author of eternal salvation unto all them that obey him; Called of God an high priest after the order of Melchisedec" Hebrews 5: 9-10

"And from Jesus Christ, who is the faithful witness, and the first begotten of the dead, and the prince of the kings of the earth. Unto him that loved us, and washed us from our sins in his own blood, And hath made us kings and priests unto God and his Father; to him be glory and dominion for ever and ever. Amen." Revelation 1:5-6

"For verily I say unto you, That whosoever shall say unto this mountain, Be thou removed, and be thou cast into the sea; and shall not doubt in his heart, but shall believe that those things which he saith shall come to pass; he shall have whatsoever he saith." Mark 11:23

"And if children, then heirs—heirs of God and joint heirs with Christ, if indeed we suffer with *Him*, that we may also be glorified together." Romans 8:17

"Jesus Christ the same yesterday, and to day, and for ever." Hebrews 13:8

"A thousand shall fall at thy side, and ten thousand at thy right hand; but it shall not come nigh thee." Psalm 91:7
"To whom God would make known what is the riches of the glory of this mystery among

the Gentiles; which is Christ in you, the hope of glory:" Colossians 1: 27

"They that trust in the LORD shall be as mount Zion, which cannot be removed, but abideth for ever." Psalm 125:1

"But Christ as a son over his own house; whose house are we, if we hold fast the confidence and the rejoicing of the hope firm unto the end. " Hebrews 3:6

"Neither is there salvation in any other: for there is none other name under heaven given among men, whereby we must be saved." Acts 4: 12

"Lo, children are an heritage of the LORD: and the fruit of the womb is his reward." Psalm 127:3

"Thou wilt keep him in perfect peace, whose mind is stayed on thee: because he trusteth in thee." Isaiah 26:3

"For thou shalt eat the labour of thine hands: happy shalt thou be, and it shall be well with thee. Thy wife shall be as a fruitful vine by the sides of thine house: thy children like olive plants round about thy table." Psalm 128:2,3

Declare the Word and take hold of it. It has staying

power. Jesus said "If you live in Me [abide vitally united to Me] and My words remain in you and continue to live in your hearts, ask whatever you will, and it shall be done for you" John 15:7(AMP).

You must confess the finished works of Jesus Christ. Declare that He is seated at the right hand of God the Father; that He came so that you might have life and have it to the full. "The thief cometh not, but for to steal, and to kill, and to destroy: I am come that they might have life, and that they might have it more abundantly" John 10:10

Now that you are born again, sin has no place in you. Jesus became sin so that you might become the righteousness of God. The Bible says you are bought with a price; therefore glorify God in your body and your spirit, which are God's. 1 Corinthians 6:12 (paraphrased). The promises of God are for you to live a glorious Christ-like life; life of victory, health, abundance, joy, faith, love, peace, kindness, and acting on your liberty to live happy and fulfilled in Christ Jesus. Stand fast therefore on your liberty in Christ. Galatians 5:1

The Word of God is Spirit and life. This Word in your mouth and heart will produce dynamic results. It will never fail or return void.

Chapter 4

DECLARING SCRIPTURES

*"It is the spirit that quickeneth; the flesh
profiteth nothing: the words that I speak
unto you, they are spirit, and they are life".*
John 6:63

*Y*ou study the Word so that you may develop
and mature spiritually. Do you finally stop studying? Not
except you become tired of living. This Word is your
necessary food. You meditate on the word till He has
dominion over you; your body, your mind and over your
whole system. Whatever you want to create or change
can only be done through the Word.

Gen 24:1   "And Abraham was old, and well stricken in
age: and the LORD had blessed Abraham in
all things.
I am blessed, that means that I am
empowered to prosper. The seed of

blessing has been passed on me. The blessings of Abraham have come upon me and my family.

Gen 13: 2   "And Abram was very rich in cattle, in silver, and in gold."

Gal 3: 6   "Even as Abraham believed God, and it was accounted to him for righteousness."

2 Cor5:17   "Therefore if any man be in Christ, he is a new creature: old things are passed away; behold all things are become new.
I have the ability to enjoy my spiritual blessings.

Num 23:23a "Surely there is no enchantment with or against Jacob; neither is there any divination with or against Israel.
I cannot be cursed because every curse is reversed.

Spiritual Development

The Word of God brings health and life to my body and transforms the circumstances of my life. Jesus Christ, the faithful and trustworthy witness who loved us and transformed us into a Kingdom, a royal race, and made us priests to our God and Father. To Him be the glory, the power, the majesty and dominion throughout all the ages. Amen.

Rev. 1:5, 6 "And from Jesus Christ, who is the faithful witness, and the first begotten of the dead, and the prince of the kings of the earth. Unto him that loved us, and washed us from our sins in his own blood, And hath made us kings and priests unto God and his Father; to him be glory and dominion for ever and ever. Amen."

Eph 5:18-19 "And be not drunk with wine, wherein is excess; but be filled with the Spirit; Speaking to yourselves in psalms and hymns and spiritual songs, singing and making melody in your heart to the Lord."

James 1: 21 "Wherefore lay apart all filthiness and superfluity of naughtiness, and receive with meekness the engrafted word, which is able to save your souls."

Psa 45: 1 "My heart is inditing a good matter: I speak of the things which I have made touching the king: my tongue is the pen of a ready writer."

Eternal Life

Eternal life is at work in me. I am the custodian of this gospel of life which encapsulates His saving power. I do not keep this gospel to myself. I tell it out.

2 Tim 4:2   "Preach the word; be instant in season, out of season; reprove, rebuke exhort with all long suffering and doctrine."

Eph 2: 10   "For we are his workmanship, created in Christ Jesus unto good works, which God hath before ordained that we should walk in them."

John 15:4   "Remain in me, and I will remain in you. No branch can bear fruit by itself; it must remain in the vine. Neither can you bear fruit unless you remain in me." **(NKJV)**

2 Cor10:4-5   "(For the weapons of our warfare are not carnal, but mighty through God to the pulling down of strong holds;) Casting down imaginations, and every high thing that exalteth itself against the knowledge of God, and bringing into captivity every thought to the obedience of Christ;"

Eph 4:14,15   "That we henceforth be no more children, tossed to and fro, and carried about with every wind of doctrine, by the sleight of men, and cunning craftiness, whereby they lie in wait to deceive; But speaking the truth in love, may grow up into him in all things, which is the head, even Christ."

Prov 4:20-22   "My son, attend to my words; incline thine ear unto my sayings. Let them not depart from thine eyes; keep them in the midst of thine heart. For they are life unto those that find them, and health to all their flesh."

2 John 5:12 "He that hath the Son hath life; and he that hath not the Son of God hath not life."

The Love Nature of Christ

I am full of love. I walk in love everyday. I refuse to condescend to the low level of hatred and malice because I live in the high realms of love where God lives. The love of God is shed abroad in my heart by the Holy Ghost. The more I demonstrate the more the power of God's anointing is released in my life.

Roms 5:5 "And hope maketh not ashamed; because the love of God is shed abroad in our hearts by the Holy Ghost which is given unto us".

Roms 8:38,39 "For I am persuaded, that neither death, nor life, nor angels, nor principalities, nor powers, nor things present, nor things to come, nor height, nor depth, nor any other creature, shall be able to separate us from the love of God, which is in Christ Jesus our Lord."

Cols 3:3 "For ye are dead, and your life is hid with Christ in God."

2 Cor 5:14 "For the love of Christ constraineth us; because we thus judge, that if one died for all, then were all dead:"

Supply: God's Provision For Me

Phils 4:19 "But my God shall supply all your need according to his riches in glory by Christ Jesus."

1 John 5:4 "For whatsoever is born of God overcometh the world: and this is the victory that overcometh the world, even our faith."

Roms 8: 1 "There is therefore now no condemnation to me who is in Christ Jesus, who walk not after the flesh but after the Spirit who has made me free from the law of sin and death."

Healing Scriptures

Because Christ is in me, my body is dead because of sin and my spirit is alive because of righteousness. The Spirit of Him that raised up Jesus from the dead dwells in me and He that raised up Christ from the dead quickens my mortal body by His spirit that dwells in me.

Roms 8:10,11 "And if Christ be in you, the body is dead because of sin; but the Spirit is life because of righteousness. But if the Spirit of him that raised up Jesus from the dead dwell in you, he that raised up Christ from the dead shall also quicken your mortal bodies by his Spirit that dwelleth in you".

Jer 30: 17 "For I will restore health unto thee, and I will heal thee of thy wounds, saith the LORD; because they called thee an Outcast, saying, This is Zion, whom no man seeketh after." **The Lord has restored health to me and has healed me of my wounds and pains.**

3 John 2 "Beloved, I wish above all things that thou mayest prosper and be in health, even as thy soul prospereth." **I prosper and I'm in health even as my soul prospers because this is God's desire for me.**

1 Tim 4:8 "For bodily exercise profiteth little: but godliness is profitable unto all things, having promise of the life that now is, and of that which is to come."

Psa 42:11b "Hope thou in God: for I shall yet praise him, who is the health of my countenance, and my God."

Phil 1:20 "According to my earnest expectation and my hope, that in nothing I shall be ashamed, but that with all boldness, as always, so now also Christ shall be magnified in my body, whether it be by life, or by death."

Prbs 3: 7-8 "Be not wise in thine own eyes: fear the

LORD, and depart from evil. It shall be health to thy navel, and marrow to thy bones."
I am not wise in my own eyes. I fear the Lord and depart from evil and this brings health to me navel and marrow to my bones.

Isa 57:18   "I have seen his ways, and will heal him: I will lead him also, and restore comforts unto him and to his mourners."

Psa 147:3   "He healeth the broken in heart, and bindeth up their wounds."
He heals my heart and binds my wounds.

Luke 13:16   "And ought not this woman, being a daughter of Abraham, whom Satan hath bound, lo these eighteen years, be loosed from this bond on the sabbath day?"
I am a seed of Abraham and it is my birth right to be healed.

Ex 23:25   "And ye shall serve the LORD your God, and he shall bless thy bread, and thy water; and I will take sickness away from the midst of thee."
I serve the Lord and He blesses my bread and my water; and He has taken away sickness from my midst.

Ex 15:26   "...I will put none of these diseases upon thee, which I have brought upon the

Egyptians: for I am the LORD that healeth thee."
I diligently hearken to the voice of the Lord my God and I do that which is right in his sight and will give ear to his commandments and keep all his statues. No disease will come on me for He is the Lord that heals me.

Psa 103:2, 3 "Bless the LORD, O my soul, and forget not all his benefits: Who forgiveth all thine iniquities; who healeth all thy diseases;"
I bless the Lord and I do not forget His benefits; because He forgives my iniquities and heals all my diseases.

Isa 33:24 "And the inhabitant shall not say I am sick: the people that dwell therein shall be forgiven their iniquity."
I do not say I am sick because I am an inhabitant of Zion.

Prbs 12:18 "There is that speaketh like the piercing of a sword: but the tongue of the wise is health."
My tongue is wise and it is health to me.

Matt 10:1 "And when he had called unto him his twelve disciples, he gave them power against unclean spirits, to cast them out, and to heal all manner of sickness and all manner of disease."

James 5:15 "And the prayer of faith shall save the sick, and the Lord shall raise him up; and if he have committed sins, they shall be forgiven him."

Psa 30:2 "O LORD my God, I cried unto thee, and thou hast healed me."
I call to the Lord and He healed me.

Gal 3:29 "And if ye be Christ's, then are ye Abraham's seed, and heirs according to the promise."
I am Abraham's seed and an heir according to the promise, therefore the promise of divine health and healing is mine.

1 Pet 2:24 "Who his own self bare our sins in his own body on the tree that we, being dead to sins, should live unto righteousness: by whose stripes ye were healed."
Christ bore my sins in his own body on the tree so that I, being dead to sin should live unto righteousness, by His stripes I am healed.

Mal 4:2 "But unto you that fear my name shall the Sun of righteousness arise with healing in his wings; and ye shall go forth, and grow up as calves of the stall."

Mark 16:17 "And these signs shall follow them that believe; In my name shall they cast out devils; they shall speak with new tongues;"

Heb 4:12 "For the word of God is quick, and powerful, and sharper than any twoedged sword, piercing even to the dividing asunder of soul and spirit, and of the joints and marrow, and is a discerner of the thoughts and intents of the heart.

1 John 3:8 "He that committeth sin is of the devil; for the devil sinneth from the beginning. For this purpose the Son of God was manifested, that he might destroy the works of the devil."

Ezk 47:9 "And it shall come to pass, that everything that liveth, which moveth, whithersoever the rivers shall come, shall live: and there shall be a very great multitude of fish, because these waters shall come thither: for they shall be healed; and every thing shall live whither the river cometh."

Rs 8:37 "Nay, in all these things we are more than conquerors through him that loved us."

Phil 4:13 "I can do all things through Christ which strengtheneth me."

1 John 5:4 "For whatsoever is born of God overcometh the world: and this is the victory that overcometh the world, even our faith."

2 Cor 4:18 "While we look not at the things which are seen, but at the things which are not seen: for the things which are seen are temporal;

but the things which are not seen are eternal."

Roms 8:11 "But if the Spirit of him that raised up Jesus from the dead dwell in you, he that raised up Christ from the dead shall also quicken your mortal bodies by his Spirit that dwelleth in you."

Eph 1:7 "In whom we have redemption through his blood, the forgiveness of sins, according to the riches of his grace;"

Matt 10:8 "Heal the sick, cleanse the lepers, raise the dead, cast out devils: freely ye have received, freely give."

Luke 10:19 "Behold, I give unto you power to tread on serpents and scorpions, and over all the power of the enemy: and nothing shall by any means hurt you."

Chapter 5

CONFESSIONS FOR LIVING

I Am Blessed

- I am blessed, that means that I am empowered to prosper. The seed of blessing has been passed on me. The blessings of Abraham have come upon me and my family. (**Gen.13: 2, Gen. 24: 1 Gal. 3:6, 19**)

- I have the ability to enjoy my spiritual blessings. The divine nature of God is manifested in me so I cannot be cursed. I have become a new person by virtue of my new birth in Christ Jesus.

- Every curse is reversed. There is no curse, enchantment or divination that can work against me. **(Numbers 23: 23)**

- My God makes me flourish like the palm trees and the cedars of Lebanon. I am like a tree planted by the rivers and my leaves are evergreen. I am making necessary investments in my personality; I'm making the world around me better than I met it.

- I cannot have a sad day because where I live is glorious. My mind is where God stays. My mind is where God seeks to work. I hail from Him, I hail from Zion. My day is full of happiness; my day is full of productivity. I am going somewhere to happen. I thank God for my victories, He is in me always even onto the end of the world. I celebrate His goodness in me daily.

Spiritual Development

- The Word of God has creative power to transform my life. It brings health and life to my body and transforms the circumstances of my life.

- Jesus Christ the faithful and trustworthy witness loved me and transformed me into a member of his Kingdom, made me part of a royal race, and presented me as a priest to our God and Father. To Him be the glory, the power, the majesty and dominion throughout all the ages. Amen. **(Rev 1:5, 6)**

- I have put away all filthy communications from my mouth. All that proceeds from my mouth edifies and ministers grace to those who hear me and brings glory to God. I am filled with the Spirit, speaking to myself in Psalms, hymns and spiritual songs. I am singing and making melody in my heart to the Lord. **(Eph 5:18, 19)**

- I am a product of many meetings. I receive with meekness the engrafted Word of God, which is able to save my soul. **(James 1: 21)**

- My heart is indicting a good matter and my tongue is as the pen of a ready writer. I am quick to hear and do the Word of God. **(Psa 45:1)**

The Love Nature Of Christ

- I have the love nature of Christ. I am full of love. I walk in love everyday. I refuse to condemn. I refuse to condescend to the low level of hatred and malice because I live in the high realm of love where God lives. The love of God is shed abroad in my heart by the Holy Ghost. **(Roms 5:5)**

- The more I demonstrate love, the more of God's anointing that is released in my life.

- I am persuaded that neither death nor life nor angels nor principalities nor powers nor things present nor things to come nor height nor depth nor any other creature shall separate me from the love of God which is in Christ Jesus our Lord. **(Roms 8:38 - 39)**

- I walk daily in the consciousness of His love because my life is hid in Christ in God. **(Col 3:3)**

- I live a stable life. The Holy Spirit is my helper so l am rooted and grounded in love. I am teachable. I am a doer of the Word. I take to instructions gladly.

- God is my source; He is my provider. He has made me a giver. I am fruitful in every good work. I have the life of God in me.

Supply : God's Provision For Me

- I am supply conscious. My God supplies all my need according to His abundant riches in glory by Christ Jesus. **(Philippians 4:19)**

- Whatsoever is born of God overcomes the world and this is the victory that overcomes the world, even our faith. For greater is He that is in me than he that is in the world. I have the spirit of faith; therefore I speak faith; I speak faith-filled words and by this I overcome the world and its system. **(2 Corinthians 3:6)**

- I am born of God and I have overcome the world. I have world overcoming faith residing in me; Greater is He that is in me than He that is in the world. I have the Spirit of faith therefore I speak faith filled words and by this I have overcome the world and its systems. **(1 John 5:4)**

- I am an able minister of the New Covenant; not of the letter but of the Spirit, for the letter kills but the Spirit gives life. I am a living epistle of Christ; I am complete in Him which is the head of all principalities and power. **(Col 3:10)**

- But we all with open face as beholding in a glass the glory of God are changed into the same image. For we have this treasure in earthen vessels, that excellence of this power may be of God and not of us. **(2 Cor 4:7)**

Our Homes

- My home is blessed. My family is blessed; my children are blessed. My family is covered; they are insured with God's Word. Sickness cannot come or stay in my home because I'm a partaker of His divine nature.

- My God is at work in my family; He is at work in me both to will and to do of His good pleasure. (Phil 2:12,13)

- He has enabled me to achieve; I'm an achiever. I can do all things through Christ who strengthens me. I am strengthened from the inside; I live from the inside out. Look at me; I live in victory. I'm more than a conqueror I am a victor. My home is blessed in Jesus' Name.

Health

- He heals all my diseases; my wounds are healed. (Jer 30:17)

- Above all things, I prosper in health even as my soul prospers. (3 John 2)

- My God forgives all of my iniquities; all my health is dependent on Him. He forgives all my iniquities and heals all my diseases. My health is dependent on His Word; I refuse to be sick. I cannot be sick. Sickness cannot stay in my body because my body is the temple of the Living God. He is in my bones, He is in my cells, and He is in my blood. He is in every fibre of my being, He dwells in me, He talks through me, and He is my lord. He is the one that heals me.

- He was wounded for my transgressions, he was bruised for my iniquities, the chastisement of my peace was upon Him and with His stripes I am healed.

- And if you be in Christ, then you are Abraham's seed and heirs according to the promise. Healing is His provision; healing is the children's bread.

- Out of my belly flow rivers of living waters. He is the vine and I'm the branch. The life of Christ flows in me. He is in every fibre of my being, in every bone of my body. I am reigning in life.

- I am born not of corruptible seed but of the seed incorruptible by the Word of God, which lives and abides forever.

Eternal Life

- Eternal life is at work in me. I am the custodian of eternal verities; I am the custodian of this gospel, which encapsulates His saving power. I do not keep this gospel to myself. I tell it out. **(2 Tim 4:2)**

- I am God's workmanship, recreated in Christ Jesus unto good works, which God has before ordained that I should walk in. I cannot be sick because I am sickness proof; I am poverty proof; I am accident proof; I am depression proof. I walking in victory because I have overcome the

world by the faith of Christ that resides inside
me.

- I am vitally connected to God by Jesus Christ;
  by the blood of Jesus.

- The Word of God is practicable. The word of
  God is for me to live by. It is life to me and
  health to my flesh. **(Proverbs 5: 22)**

- The Word vitalises every path of my body. My
  body is vitalised through the Word, my blood is
  vitalised through the Word, my heart is vitalised
  through the Word. My bones are vitalised
  through the Word and my sight is vitalised
  through the Word.

- The Word is working in me; eternal life is at
  work in me. I have received life and I enjoy it
  to the fullest. The eternal life of God is in me
  and it permeates my entire body. My spirit,
  soul and body are infused with divinity,
  therefore I cannot be sick. I cannot be sick in
  my mind, I cannot be sick in my body. I cannot
  be poor. I cannot be disadvantaged in this life.
  I live the life of heaven here on earth because
  divine life flows in me; because divine life is at
  work in me. **(2 Cor 2:14)**

- Christianity is a call to the triumphant life; that
  means I am called to live a life of consistent
  success; I am called to live a life of progress,

peace, joy, and health and of unending prosperity.

- I am excited in my spirit. I am full of joy, in me dwells the house of God. I am a power packed person. The anointing of the Holy Spirit in me is to help me do what ordinary men cannot do. It is to help me see what natural men cannot see. This is the grace of God, which is the beauty, and glory of God. This is the grace that has come over my life and separated me from the general class. **(Gen 49:28)**

- I have been separated and located and dominated and nominated by grace. Therefore I rejoice because my God has said, " I am going to give you houses you did not build." My God has said in His Word, "I will give you wells you did not dig," because I am set apart from the rest of the world by grace, by the anointing and by the Spirit of God.

- I'm functioning in revelation hence everything I do has outstanding results. **(Psalm 16:11)**

- I don't walk alone. God is perfecting my life. Failure is not consistent with my nature. Success is consistent with my nature Progress is consistent with my nature. I'm walking in advantage because I'm positioned for advantage.

- I'm confident of this very thing, that he who has begun a good work in me, will perform to the day of Jesus Christ. **(Philippians 1:6)**

- I am walking in paths prepared for me ahead of time and my footsteps will not slide. **(Eph 2:10)**

Peace

- My God keeps me in peace; I am dwelling in the rest of God, in strength and salvation. I am a worshipper; I never let the praise of God depart from my mouth. **(Matthew 21: 6)**

- Oh hear me sing for my God is great. He has given me a lovely voice to praise him for His goodness overshadows me.

- I do not have the spirit of fear but of love, of power and of a sound mind. I HAVE A SOUND MIND! The lines are falling for me in pleasant places; I have a goodly heritage. The deeds of darkness are completely removed from my life for there is no darkness in His Kingdom, so fear cannot stay in me. It is impossible for fear to stay in me. Victory lives in me. I live in peace, prosperity and divine health all the days of my life; therefore my heart is at rest and I have no reason to fret anymore for I am super abundantly provided for in Jesus name. Amen.

- I am cool, I'm happy, I sleep well for my God sits in the heavens and laughs because He sees me walking relaxed, and there is no stress in my life. I'm walking in victory, I'm walking in His spirit.

- I am blessed with peace that gives rest. I live a trouble free life and give no place to worries I have joy everlasting. I'm full of glory for the joy of the Lord is my strength. I have entered into his rest and I have ceased from my struggles I am anxious for nothing and have joy everlasting. (John 14: 27)

Conclusion

RECEIVE THE WORD

"Heaven and earth shall
pass away: but my words
shall not pass away."
Mark 13: 31

The Word of God can be received or rejected. The attitude with which you receive the word is important. It can be received with doubt or faith and appreciation. The Bible says "Receive with meekness the engrafted word" James 1:21.

The Word of God is a gift from God for all saints. The Word is our food and source of life, which must be enjoyed, heard, read, believed and received to accomplish its purpose for us. The Word is effective but cannot function in an environment of doubt and unbelief, neither can it function when it is confessed with fear or double mindedness.

"For this cause also thank we God without ceasing, because, when ye received the word of God which ye heard of us, ye received it not as the word of men, but as it is in truth, the word of God, which effectually worketh also in you that believe." 1 Thessalonians 2:13

It is beautiful when we make the Word our priority by letting the Word dwell in us richly. The Bible says *"Let the word of Christ dwell in you richly in all wisdom; teaching and admonishing one another in psalms and hymns and spiritual songs, singing with grace in your hearts to the Lord."* Colossians 3:16

When you dedicate our mouths to celebrate God's Word, you are committed to uttering words of faith, words of joy, words of power and victory, words of love and grace and words of life, God's ability is released in you.

"Thus saith the LORD, the Holy One of Israel, and his Maker, Ask me of things to come concerning my sons, and concerning the work of my hands command ye me." Isaiah 45:11

"Blessed be the LORD my strength which teacheth my hands to war, and my fingers to fight:" Psalm 144:1

"Ask me and I will tell you remarkable secrets you do not know about things to come" Jeremiah 33:3 (NLT)

"As the mountains are round about Jerusalem,

so the LORD is round about his people from
henceforth even for ever." Psalm 125:2

"Fear thou not; for I am with thee: be not
dismayed; for I am thy God: I will strengthen
thee; yea, I will help thee; yea, I will uphold
thee with the right hand of my righteousness."
Isaiah 41: 10

"Surely goodness and mercy shall follow me
all the days of my life: and I will dwell in the
house of the LORD for ever." Psalm 23:6

"And I saw heaven opened, and behold a white horse;
and he that sat upon him was called Faithful and True,
and in righteousness he doth judge and make war.
His eyes were as a flame of fire, and on his head were
many crowns; and he had a name written, that no
man knew, but he himself. And he was clothed with a
vesture dipped in blood: and his name is called
The Word of God." Romans 19:11-13

Pgadmissions=exrel @ salford.ac.uk
0161 - 295 - 3306 /5641

871 968 6921
$950 =>

=> Sandra Uadiale =>
=> Name of Piece —— Deda
=> 1900 South Missouri Street
    Casper —— Wyoming
=> 82609 / USA